children's book of

Classic Catholic Prayers

EDITED BY

ROBERT F. MORNEAU

ILLUSTRATIONS BY

DENNIS ROCKHILL

Paulist Press

New York/Mahwah, N.J.

Cover illustration by Dennis Rockhill
Cover design by Therese Borchard

Library of Congress Cataloging-in-Publication Data

Children's book of classic Catholic prayers / edited by Robert F. Morneau ; illustrations by Dennis Rockhill.
p. cm.
Summary: An illustrated collection of prayers in the Catholic tradition.
ISBN 0-8091-6666-6 (alk. paper)
1. Catholic Church--Prayer-books and devotions--English. 2. Children--Prayer-books and devotions--English. [1. Catholic Church--Prayer books and devotions. 2. Prayer books and devotions. 3. Prayers.] I. Morneau, Robert F., 1938– II. Rockhill, Dennis, ill.

BX1981 .C45 1999
242′.682 21--dc21 99-041548
CIP

Published by Paulist Press
997 Macarthur Boulevard
Mahwah, New Jersey 07430

www.paulistpress.com

Printed and bound in the United States of America.

To the Most Reverend Aloysius J. Wycislo, D.D.
Bishop Emeritus of Green Bay, Wisconsin
—R. F. M.

To my family, especially Sue and Autumn,
for your sacrifice of husband and daddy time.
And to SCOB and Butterfly, my family-in-writing.
—D. R.

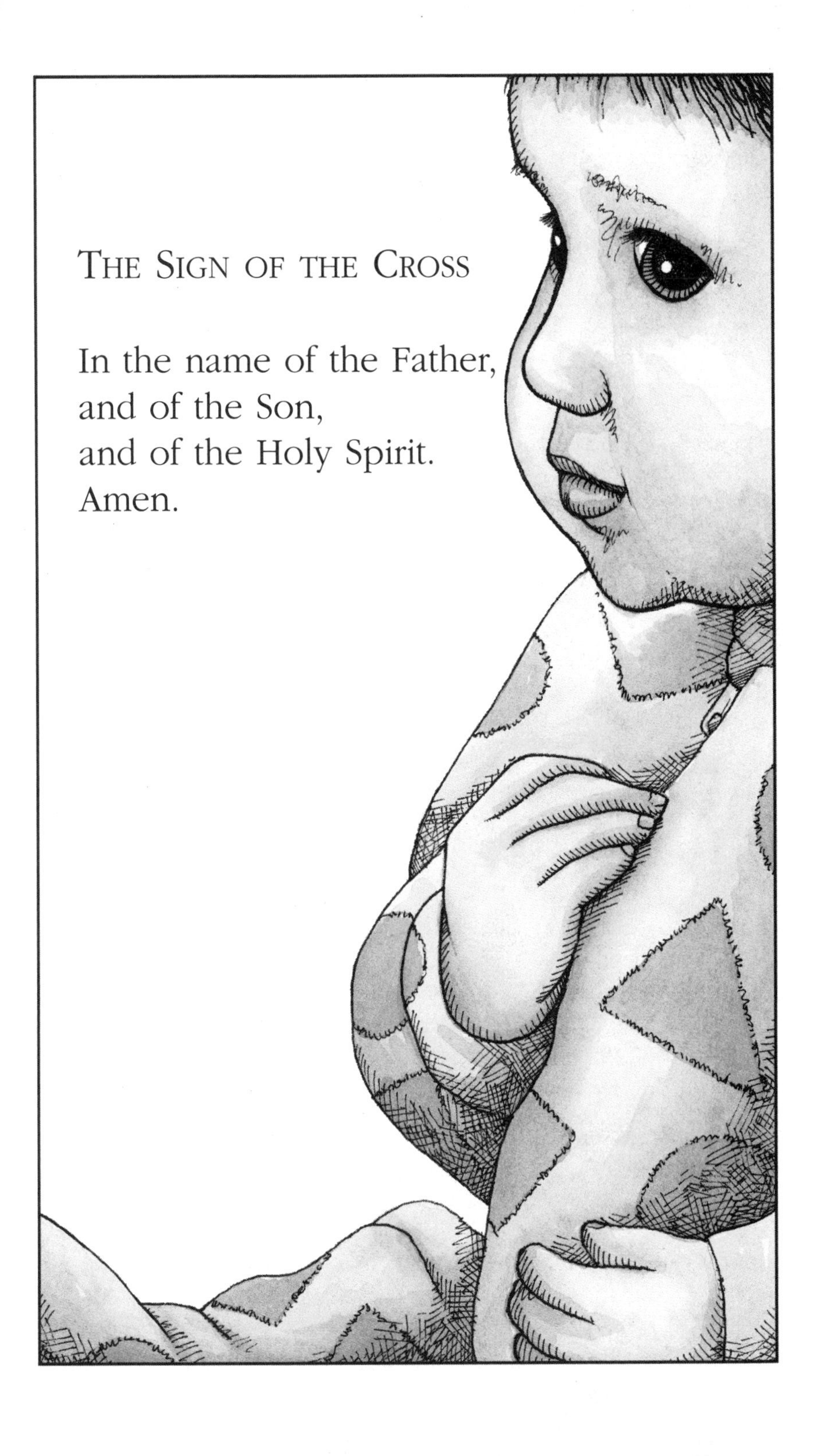

THE SIGN OF THE CROSS

In the name of the Father,
and of the Son,
and of the Holy Spirit.
Amen.

THE LORD'S PRAYER

Our Father,
who art in heaven,
hallowed be thy name;
thy kingdom come;
thy will be done on earth
as it is in heaven.

Give us this day our daily bread;
and forgive us our trespasses,
as we forgive those that trespass
against us;
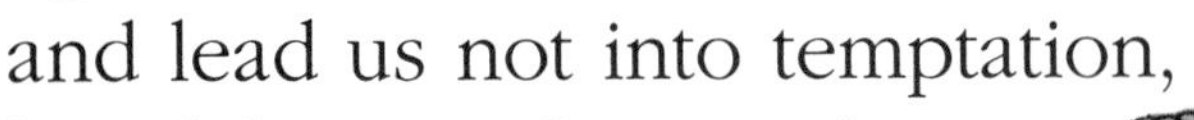
and lead us not into temptation,
but deliver us from evil.
Amen.

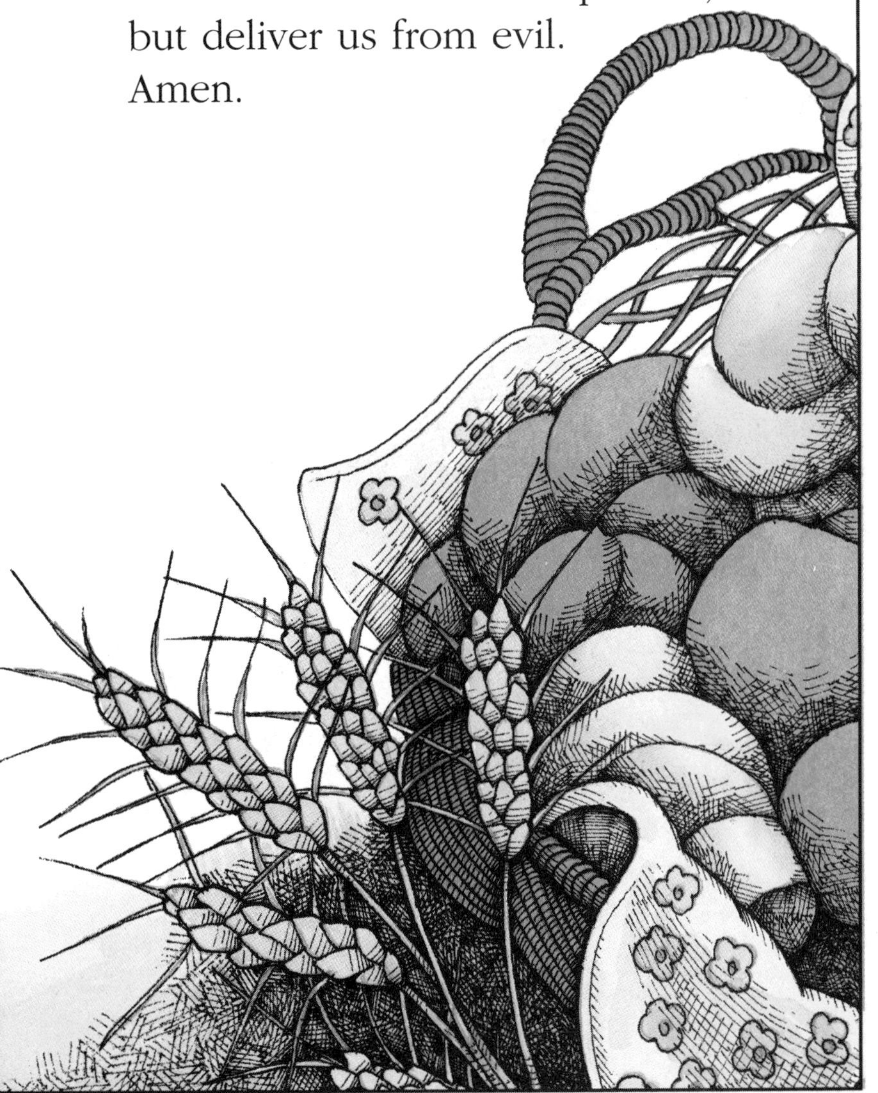

The Hail Mary

Hail Mary, full of grace,
the Lord is with thee.
Blessed art thou
among women,
and blessed is the fruit
of thy womb, Jesus.
Holy Mary, Mother of God,
Pray for us sinners, now,
and at the hour of our death.
Amen.

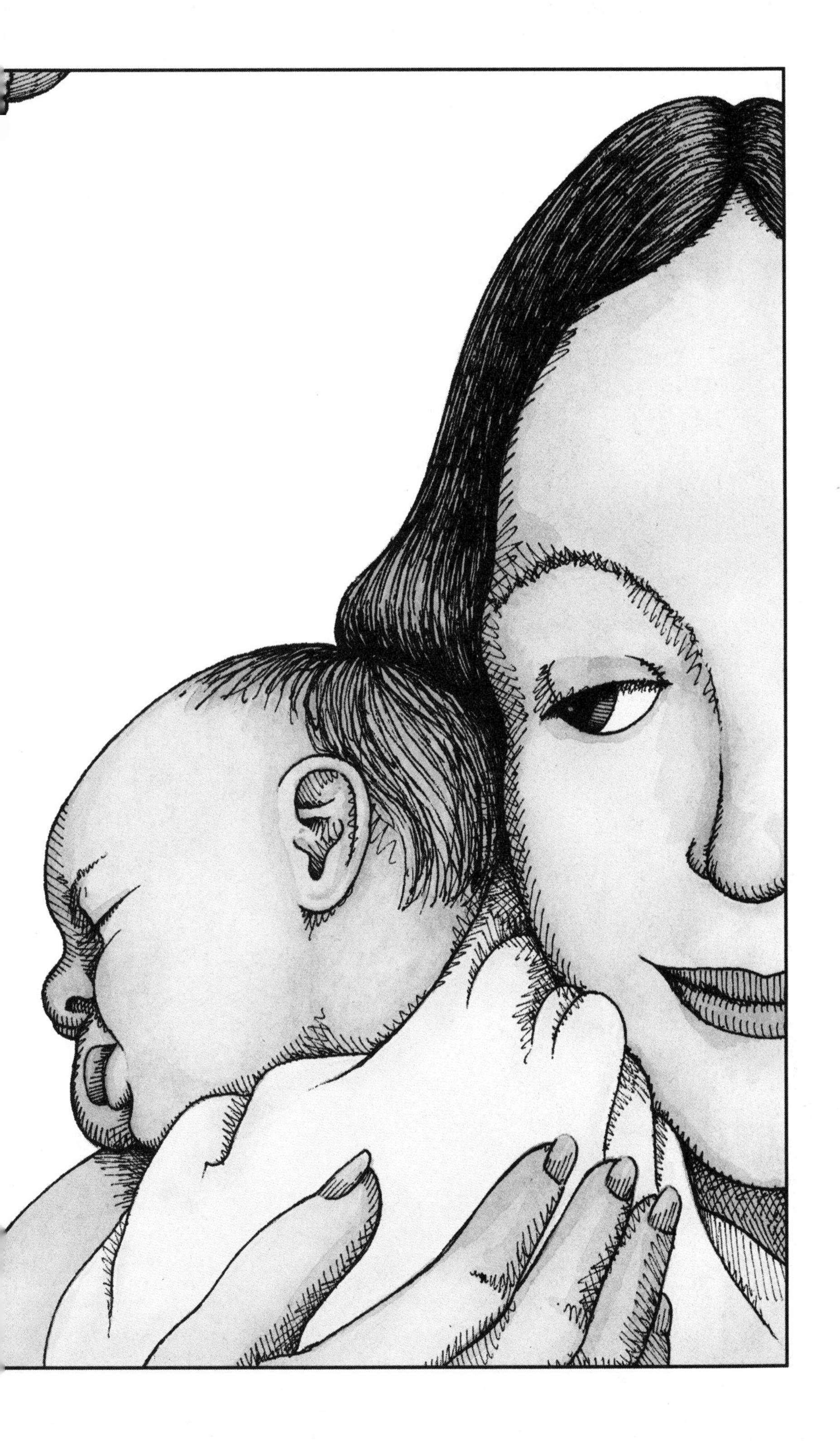

The Glory Be

Glory be to the Father
and to the Son
and to the Holy Spirit.
As it was in the beginning
is now and ever shall be
world without end.
Amen.

Prayer to the Holy Spirit

Come, Holy Spirit,
and fill our hearts
with the fire of your love.
Amen.

The Apostles' Creed

I believe in God,
the Father almighty,
creator of heaven and earth.
I believe in Jesus Christ,
his only Son, our Lord.
He was conceived by the power
of the Holy Spirit
and born of the Virgin Mary.
He suffered under Pontius Pilate,
was crucified, died,
and was buried.
He descended into hell.
On the third day he rose again.
He ascended into heaven
and is seated at the right hand
of the Father.
He will come again
to judge the living and the dead.
I believe in the Holy Spirit,
the holy catholic church,
the communion of saints,
the forgiveness of sins,
the resurrection of the body,
and life everlasting. Amen.

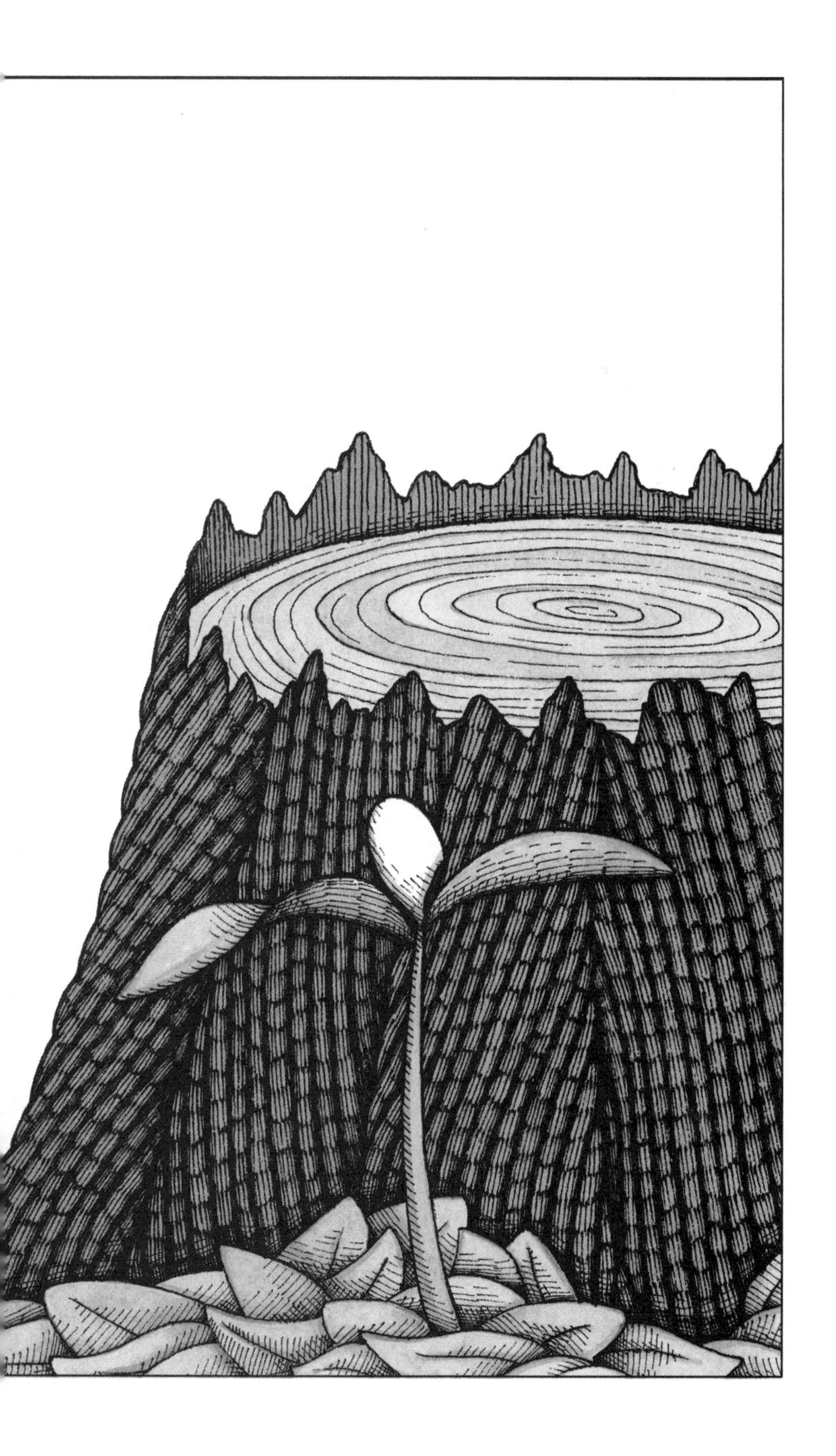

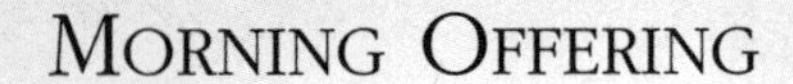

Morning Offering

O Jesus,
I offer you all the prayers,
thoughts, works,
and sufferings of this day.
Grant, O Lord,
that no one may love you less
this day because of me;
that no word or action of mine
may turn a soul from you;
and that many souls
will love you more this day
because of me.
Amen.

Act of Faith

My God, I believe that you
are one God
in three divine persons:
Father, Son and Holy Spirit.
I believe you are the creator
of all things.
I believe that your son, Jesus,
came among us as a man.
He suffered and died
for our sins,
but rose again from the dead
on the third day.
I believe that you sent
the Holy Spirit among us.
I believe these things and all
that your holy Catholic Church
teaches us.
Amen.

Act of Hope

My God, I hope
and trust in you
and I believe in all
of your promises
because you sent us
your son, Jesus,
who will bring us
closer to you.
Amen.

Act of Love

My God, I love you
above all things
because you are all good.
I love you as the creator of life,
I love you as the one
who has forgiven our sins
and opened the gates of heaven.
I love you as the Spirit
whom you have sent among us
to guide us in this world.
Because of my love for you,
I love my neighbor as myself.
Amen.

Act of Contrition

O Lord Jesus,
I am truly sorry for all my sins
because they caused you pain
and sorrow on the cross;
and with your help,
my good and loving Savior,
I will always love you
and never sin again.
Amen.

The Confiteor

I confess to Almighty God,
and to you my brothers
and sisters,
that I have sinned
through my own fault,
in my thoughts
and in my words,
in what I have done,
and in what I have failed to do;
and I ask blessed Mary,
ever virgin,
all the angels and saints,
and you, my brothers and sisters,
to pray for me
to the Lord our God.
Amen.

Grace before Meals

Bless us, O Lord,
and these your gifts,
which we are about to receive
from your goodness,
through Christ our Lord.
Amen.

Grace after Meals

We give you thanks,
Almighty God,
for these and all the gifts
we have received
from your goodness,
through Christ our Lord.
Amen.

Prayer for the Home

Lord, visit this house
and family,
and drive away
all evil and harm.
Let your angels dwell
in our home
and let your blessing
live among us.
Amen.

Evening Prayer
Now I lay me down to sleep.
I pray the Lord my soul to keep.
If I should die before I wake,
I pray the Lord my soul to take.

Prayer of St. Francis

Lord, make me an instrument
of your peace.
Where there is hatred,
let me sow love;
Where there is injury, pardon;
Where there is doubt, faith;
Where there is despair, hope;
Where there is darkness, light;
Where there is sadness, joy.

O Divine Master, grant that I
may not so much seek
to be consoled, as to console;
To be understood,
as to understand;
To be loved, as to love.
For it is in giving that we receive;
It is in pardoning
that we are pardoned;
And it is in dying
that we are born to eternal life.
Amen.

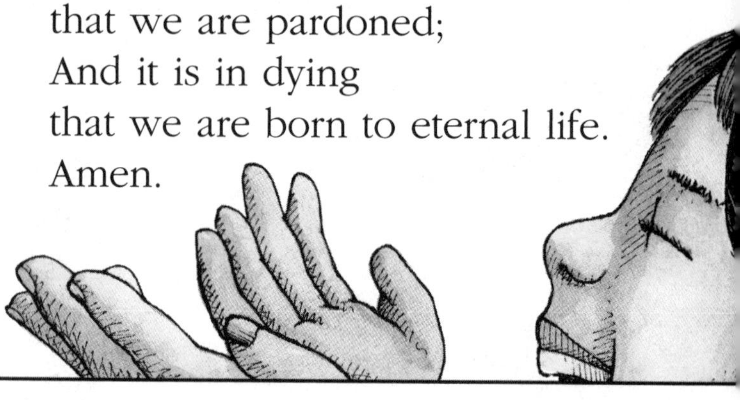

Prayer to Mary

Remember, O Mary,
that you have always helped
every soul who has begged
for your mercy.
We come before you,
our Mother,
trusting that you will hear
our petitions and answer us.
Amen.

GUARDIAN ANGEL
Angel of God,
my guardian dear,
to whom God's love
commits me here,
ever this day be at my side,
to light and guard,
to rule and guide.
Amen.

Prayer to St. Joseph

Good Saint Joseph,
we praise and honor you
as the foster father of Jesus
and the husband of Mary.
As protector of the Holy Family,
pray for us to Jesus,
your foster child.
Keep us close to the heart of Jesus
so that we come safely home
to heaven to be with you
and Mary and all the saints.
Amen.

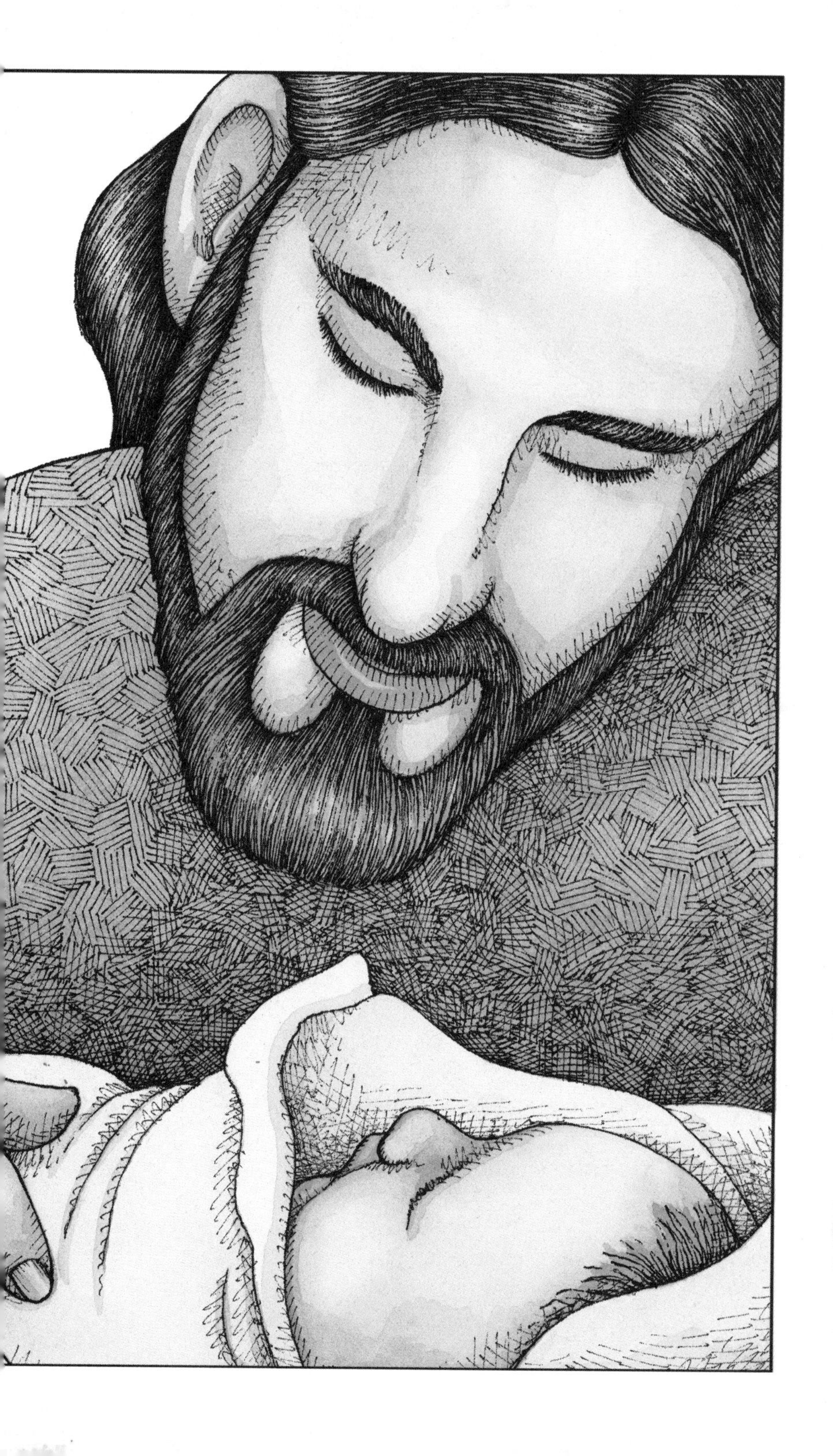